Exploring the Soul of *Taharah*

iv

ב"ה

Exploring the Soul
of
Taharah

Rabbi Avivah W. Erlick, BCC

Richard A. Light

Copyright © 2015 Avivah W. Erlick and Richard A. Light

All rights reserved. No part of this book may be reproduced or transmitted in any form by any means, electronic or mechanical, including photocopying, recording, or by any information storage and retrieval system, without express permission in writing from the authors. All inquiries should be addressed to **midwifingsouls@gmail.com**.

ISBN-13: 978-1508412366
ISBN-10: 1508412367

Cover photo: Richard Moeller
Cover and book design: Richard A. Light

Acknowledgements

The authors would like to thank our teacher and friend, David Zinner, Executive Director of *Kavod v'Nichum*, for inspiring this project, and for encouraging us to develop this teaching.

Dedication

Avivah dedicates this book, "to my beloved husband, Jay, for everything."

Rick dedicates this book to Dan Tanaka, who in a moment of innocence demonstrated to all of us how holy this work really is. Thanks, Dan.

Contents

Acknowledgements vii
Dedication viii
Contents ix
Preface 1
Introduction 3
    Taharah Basics 6
        · A Series of Ritual Actions 6
        · Gestures of Ritual 7
        · Symbolic Words 8
        · Spiritual Intent 8
        · Safety 9
    An Ancient Rite 11
    Foundations of Family-Centered *Taharah* 14
    Taharah Manuals, Ancient and Modern 18

Classic *Taharah* 21
    Traditional Motivations 23
    The Role of the Traditional *Rosh* 25
    Traditional *Taharah* Boundaries 27

Family-Centered Jewish Washing Ceremonies 31
    Family-Centered Motivations 33
    Halachah and *Taharah* 35
    The Role of the Family-Centered *Rosh* 39
    Family-Centered Ceremony Boundaries 41
        · Religion of the *Meit* 41
        · Religion of Participants 42
        · Modesty Issues 43
        · Non-Traditional Practices 44
        · A Pretty Picture 45
        · Beyond Jewish Bounds 46

A Nice Jewish Question 49
About the Authors 50
About Kavod v'Nichum and Gamliel Institute 51
Other Books by the Authors 53
Selected Bibliography 56

$\overline{x}$

Preface

Every year since 2003, the North American Jewish community has been privileged to attend annual conferences dedicated to Jewish death-related practices, Jewish cemeteries, and related Jewish education. These conferences are well attended and have proven to be significant sources of learning and growth. They are sponsored and run by a non-profit organization called, *Kavod v'Nichum*,[1] whose executive director is David Zinner. As the 2015 conference program design began to take shape, David asked Rabbi Avivah Erlick to lead a track on "Family-Centered *Taharah*," and he asked Rick Light to lead a track on "Traditional *Taharah*." We (Avivah and Rick) decided that it would be appropriate to open the conference with a joint session discussing the differences and similarities between these two approaches to this holy rite. For that joint session, in order to better clarify our own thinking, we began to email ideas back and forth, creating a document detailing these topics and comparing the approaches. As time went on, the document grew, and before we knew it, this book was born.

This is a work in progress. There are no right or wrong answers to the questions we explore herein. We invite you to join us in this adventure, to better understand how we as Jews should appropriately honor our dead, our families, our communities, and our traditions. Your suggestions, comments, and ideas are welcome and encouraged.

---

[1] More information about *Kavod v'Nichum* appears at the back of the book.

Introduction

Among the many ritual actions that the Jewish tradition mandates upon the lives of its followers, those around death are considered the holiest. This is because they demonstrate so many of what we might call Judaism's "best practices." They are performed purely out of kindness and good will. They bring together and help maintain communities and families. And the recipients of these actions are completely dependent upon this benevolence, and they can never express their gratitude.

Judaism's rituals for responding to death are ancient and deep; beautiful, mysterious and misunderstood; filled with meaning, wonder, and kindness; and as diverse as are the communities of Jews the world over.

One of the central elements of these traditions is the ritual known as *taharah* (ritual purification), the long-established, cultural and religious ceremony of ablution by which the Jewish people prepare their dead for disposition.

Taharah is more than a ceremonial acknowledgement of a death. It is really quite surreal. It is a ritual performed through touching and dressing a dead person. By means we cannot know, it transforms the unholiest thing in life, the definitive source of impurity in the Jewish lexicon, a corpse, into one of the holiest: a ritually pure vessel and its soul ready to face God. It is a moment outside of time. And we who have experienced this need to share its magic with the greater world.

Taharah exists today because of dedicated individuals who have carried it on continuously in Jewish communities worldwide since ancient times. They have taught it to fellow practitioners, and made it available to families wishing for the "holiest possible" Jewish send-off for their loved ones. Everyone studying and performing *taharah*, as well as everyone in the Jewish community who receives this service when death occurs, owes those who have maintained the tradition a debt of gratitude.

Taharah is traditionally performed by a group of dedicated and trained personnel called a *chevrah kadisha*, literally a "holy society" or "sacred fellowship." *Taharah* involves gentle washing, spiritual purification by water, dressing and blessing of the decedent, following a fixed liturgy. It is believed that the ceremony grooms both the body and the soul for a safe journey to their final resting places in this world and the next.

Many cultures around the world have developed rituals that prepare the dead for burial or cremation. Many nurses and funeral home employees routinely wash their clients, some with kindness and sensitivity. So what differentiates *taharah*? What makes a *taharah* a *taharah*? In this volume, we seek to set out an understanding of *taharah* that we believe is a first: to define its essence, its soul.

The question of *taharah's* intrinsic definition arises because practices around this ritual are expanding. To be able to speak about today's continuum of death care rituals, including questions about which of these can be called Jewish, and which qualify as *taharah*, we will adopt some terminology.

The way things have traditionally been done in *taharah*, at least since the late 1800's with the institution of modern mortuaries in the United States and Canada, we shall call "classic *taharah*." This approach, common today among *chevrot kadisha* (burial societies) around the world, is performed with anonymity, out of sight of the family, in a mortuary prep room. It is characterized by a significant emphasis on respect for the sacredness of this ritual, creating a smooth-flowing rite, without interruptions, that is as complete and holy as possible.

The emerging alternative approach, we shall call "family-centered *taharah*." This more flexible treatment of the ritual invites into the equation the desires and needs of the dying and their circle of care (those responsible for their treatment and decision-making, legal and otherwise). The ritual can be performed in the home or facility where the person dies, as well as a mortuary. Members of the circle of care can participate. Enacting a scripted ritual is less important than creating a meaningful one for the family.

By "classic," we do not necessarily mean to suggest a link to the

Orthodox Movement. *Chevrah kadisha* members come from Hassidic, Orthodox, Conservative, Reform, Renewal and Reconstructionist congregations and communities, and can even be unaffiliated. Classic *taharah* practitioners often perform the rite as they were trained to do, inheriting a directive to strictly follow the local customs that have been in place for generations. We will use the words "classic", "conventional" and "traditional" interchangeably, but these could just as well be replaced by "typical," "customary," or "familiar."

Family-centered Jewish washing ceremonies, on the other hand, are rituals based on the tradition of *taharah*, but with more openness to modification. When death comes to Jewish families today, they may request a classic *taharah*. Or, they may turn for comfort to their Jewish hospice chaplain, rabbi, or a friend familiar with these customs, and request a ceremony adapted to suit a different set of needs. The family-centered *taharah* is a co-created, customized ritual that draws deeply from the well of classic *taharah*, while simultaneously accommodating the wishes of the family, even if these run counter to some of the traditional Jewish practices.

A commonly accepted name has not yet arisen for this approach to *taharah*, although some have called it liberal *taharah*, home *taharah*, Final Kindness (see bibliography), or Jewish-style home funeral. For the sake of this volume we will alternate between the terms family-centered *taharah*, *taharah*-like ceremonies, and Jewish washing rituals.

We will use the terms ceremony, ritual and rite interchangeably. We will adopt the plural of *chevrah kadisha* to be *chevrot kadisha* rather than the Americanized *chevrah kadishas*.

For the sake of simplicity, we will use the masculine singular in Hebrew to refer to both male and female examples, and the plural pronoun in English. Thus *meit*, meaning a (male) person who has died, will refer in all cases to both male and female decedents; and *rosh*, meaning a (male) leader, will refer to male and female supervisors; the plural is *roshim*. "They" is used to suggest both he and she.

Taharah Basics

Taharah developed in Jewish history as a response to two central priorities of Jewish life set out early in its teachings: to honor the dead (*kavod hameit*), and to comfort mourners (*nichum aveilim*).

Taharah honors the dead physically, by preparing them for burial. Ground burial, according to Jewish tradition, must occur for the soul to move on from this world to join God in the World to Come. No *meit* can bury themselves, of course; so to ready them for this transition is to perform the ultimate kindness. It is thus performed with great care and tenderness, as well as respect, modesty and dignity.

Taharah honors the dead spiritually, by use of a poetically rich liturgy that honors and acclaims the soul in transition. Just as a midwife escorts a newborn into this world, the *chevrah kadisha* escorts the unseen soul during its unsettled transition into the World to Come.

Taharah comforts the mourners, allowing the family to feel supported and affirmed. Participants in the ritual share in the family's responsibility for preparation and burial of the *meit*, and do so in a manner that acknowledges their shared Jewish heritage, and the holy, God-given nature of the human body and the life it has lived.

The following are the basic components of any *taharah* ritual.

✡ A Series of Ritual Actions

The central act of the *taharah* ceremony is the ablution by water. This is usually accomplished either by lowering the deceased into a dedicated *mikvah* (ritual bath), or by pouring the equivalent of nine *kavim* of clean water over the body in a continuous flow. (A *kav* is a Talmudic measure understood by many to be between 1.5 and 2.7 US quarts; more on this in the *Halachah* and *Taharah* chapter.)

As with any Jewish ritual ablution (such as washing the hands before eating, or the *mikvah* visit of "Jews by choice" as part of conversion), the purification is preceded by a thorough cleansing. Shampoo, soap, washcloths, combs, nail polish remover and more are used to attain a high conventional standard of cleanliness. There should be nothing preventing the ritual water from coming into contact with every square inch of the *meit*, not even knots in the hair.

After the washing and pouring, the body is dried and dressed in the traditional burial garments known as *tachrichim*, an outfit consisting of pants, shirt, jacket and head covering, made of plain white cotton or linen, and sewn without pockets, hems, knots or metal closures. Strips of fabric are tied in special knots around the clothes; the deceased is then wrapped in a prayer shawl (traditionally just for men, but available for women today) and a burial sheet, and placed in a casket.

✡ Gestures of Ritual

Taharah uses ritual, so as to impart specifically Jewish meaning to the action of washing the dead. As with any ritual, it uses gestures and objects; is performed in a sequestered place; and follows a set sequence to transmit core values. Its components are physical, emotional, spiritual and psychological; beautiful and respectful; and fall within the capability of those performing it.

Gestures characteristic of the *taharah* ritual include avoiding passing objects over the *meit*, where the *neshamah* (soul) is believed to be present, or standing near the top of the head, where the *Shekhinah* (the presence of the Divine) is believed to observe; deliberately pouring the water overhand, rather than using utensils in a "routine" manner; and tying the *tachrichim* knots in a shape similar to Hebrew letters that suggest a name of God.

The traditional *taharah* is performed in a location that is suitable for the procedure, as well as in keeping with the task, and which provides an environment supportive of the necessary *kavanah* (mindfulness or conscious intention) of participants.

✡ Symbolic Words

Taharah's most uniquely Jewish trait is its liturgy. *Taharah* manuals incorporate passages from Jewish texts, along with original compositions from their compilers (see *Taharah* Manuals, Ancient and Modern).

The intention is to connect the deceased to their Jewish heritage and to God; to engage the *taharah* team to ensure proper spiritual focus; to guide the team through the procedure at hand; and to comfort and assist the *neshamah* while it is in transition from this world to the next. The liturgy is based on Kabbalistic teachings; is intended to connect the deceased, the *taharah* team, and God through this process; and is structured to guide the group through all phases of the ritual.

✡ Spiritual Intent

Attention to the task by all participants is paramount. It is this mindfulness, coupled with the introduction of ritual elements, that transforms a mundane and potentially disturbing activity into a sublime act of loving-kindness.

An appropriate *kavanah* must be summoned by everyone present, so as to be respectful of the dignity and modesty of the *meit*. The participants should have in mind the intent to assist a soul in transition, and to perform the ritual accurately and completely to the best of their ability. No one should be permitted into the ritual space who is not fully committed to this spiritual exercise.

As Rabbi Stuart Kelman, a scholar of liturgy and dean of the Gamliel Institute, and co-author Dan Fendel note in their commentary on the *taharah* manual, the metaphors echoed in this ritual are doubly powerful. They suggest both that the *neshamah* is being honored and prepared as was the High Priest (*Kohen Gadol*) before he entered the ancient Temple in Jerusalem, and that the *neshamah* is on the same path:

> We are told that the *neshamah*, the spirit of the deceased, is in the room with us. And while we're doing what resembles Zechariah's description of the preparation of the *Kohen Gadol* to

enter the Holy of Holies, therein to meet the Divine, so that is what we're doing in relation to the *neshamah* of the deceased in front of us. We are, it can be said, preparing the deceased for two different destinations. On the one hand, we are preparing the physical part of the deceased for burial in the ground, from whence we all come. On the other hand, we are preparing the spiritual part, the *neshamah*, for an entrance into the presence of the Divine. It is essential that we keep both parts of the process in the front of our consciousness while we engage in the process of *taharah*. Our purpose is no less holy than the task that confronted those preparing the *Kohen Gadol*.[2]

We note that at the same time that participants are to focus on ensuring the ritual's completion, they should have an equal and balanced understanding that the ritual doesn't have to be "perfect" to be "right." When situations arise that prevent the team from performing all aspects of the ritual in the usual way, holding the *intention* to do this holy work, in a spirit of *kavod hameit*, provides a basis for participants to "do the best they can" under the circumstances, and this must be, and therefore *is*, enough.

Purity of intent, coupled with knowledge of the ritual, can yield a Jewish purification rite of the highest available standards, thereby comforting families to know that they have "done everything they could" for their loved one.

✡ Safety

Lastly, the procedure includes a means to protect the *taharah* team, ensuring their physical, emotional, and spiritual wellbeing. The use of personal protective clothing and equipment (such as disposable gloves, face shields, and gowns) is a must for all teams performing *taharah* on strangers, to protect them from contagious conditions.[3]

---

[2] Kelman, Stuart, and Fendel, Dan. *Chesed Shel Emet, The Truest Act of Kindness.* 3rd Edition, Berkeley, CA: EKS Publishing, 2013. Page xix.

[3] The dead carry fewer germs than the living. Most illnesses die with their host. But some conditions, such as drug-resistant staff infections like MRSA, are common among those who have recently spent time in the hospital, and can be highly contagious.

Teams may conduct briefings before and after the ritual, along with closing rituals, inviting team members to process any disturbing experiences they may have encountered in relation to or during the ritual performance.

An Ancient Rite

Washing of the dead is mentioned in the *Tanach* (Jewish Bible) and Talmud, and has always been an essential element of Jewish life. In his ethical will dated 1357, Eleazer of Mayence, Germany, wrote:

> I beg of you, my sons and daughters, my wife, and all of the congregation, that no funeral oration be spoken in my honor. Do not carry my body on a bier, but in a coach. Wash me clean, comb my hair, trim my nails, as I was want to do in my lifetime, so that I may go clean to my eternal rest, as I went clean to synagogue every Sabbath–day. If the ordinary officials dislike the duty, let adequate payment be made to some poor man who shall render this service carefully and not perfunctorily.[4]

The ritual as we know it, however, was an outgrowth of the development of *chevrot kadisha*, the community charitable organizations charged with caring for the sick, dying, and all matters relating to death. These arose in Jewish communities during the Middle Ages as a normative part of communal culture.

According to Professor Jacob R. Marcus, death care "brotherhoods" first formed in Spain as early as the 13th century, possibly basing their liturgy on the works of Nachmanides (d. ca. 1270), who summarized the laws concerning the sick and the dying in his book *Torat HaAdam*.

After the Jews of Spain were expelled in 1492, they took this custom with them across Europe and to Palestine, where the Jewish mystical school known as *Kabbalah* underwent a revival in the 16th and 17th centuries. Inherent in its teachings are an acute interest in death, and a will to develop original liturgies for Jewish customs that incorporate mystical teachings. To quote Marcus:

> Spain gave basic organizational form and social content; Palestine, in a supplementary sense, supplied spiritual content. The two ideas met and merged in Italy and the new death-bed liturgy was introduced into the workings of the societies. ... These detailed liturgies, similar to those which had long been

---

[4] Marcus, Jacob R.: *The Jew in the Medieval World, a Sourcebook: 315–1791*. Atheneum, New York, 1979. Page 316.

characteristic of the Catholic Church and of the Christian confraternities, were best carried out by a group, a burial Brotherhood.[5]

The oldest extant *taharah* manual, the *Ma'avor Yabok*, was compiled by Aaron Berechiah ben Moshe of Modena, and published in 1626 in Mantua, Italy. Full of mystical meanings and spiritual teachings, it remains the backbone of the *taharah* ritual as performed across North America, and much of the Jewish world, today.[6]

In the centuries since, the *taharah* ritual has been carried on without fanfare by committed individuals passing it from generation to generation. And, over time, those retaining this ritual became hard to find. As Rabbi Elchanon Zohn, Jewish death scholar and *rosh* of a large New York City *chevrah kadisha*, points out:

> What happened in this country that for many years the *chevrah* was less than respected, often ridiculed and largely ignored? Why was the *chevrah* generally perceived by the funeral director as an outside group to be called in at a time of necessity, only when insisted upon by the family, the Rabbi, the Society, or the cemetery? Respect for the *chevrah kadisha* as an institution, appreciation for the beauty of its customs, interest in its meaning to the Jewish community declined to a great extent. I dare say, that even within the most traditional quarters of the Jewish community, there was a loss of respect and appreciation for the work of the *chevrah*, whose members often downplayed and denied their participation.[7]

The reasons some offer for the decline in centrality of the *chevrah kadisha* include the popularization of the for-profit American funeral home, and a concurrent move among the Jewish public away from

---

[5] Marcus, Jacob R. *Communal Sick-Care in the German Ghetto*. Hebrew Union College Press, 1978. Pp. 65-67.

[6] As demonstrated in discussions and presentations at international *chevrah kadisha* conferences over the past decade. The procedure followed most often in Israel today differs slightly, following the writings of Gaon Harav Yechiel Tucazinsky, author of *Gesher HaChaim*, Jerusalem, 1949.

[7] Zohn, Elchanon. *Respect For a Sacred Society*. Website article from http://uhcofny.com/fs.htm

esoteric practices that separated them from their neighbors. As Jews migrated to the West to get away from anti-Semitism, it was natural for them to want to blend into their new society. One result of this was a desire to let others take care of the dead. Thus, *taharah* was carried on until recent decades almost exclusively in isolated Orthodox Jewish circles. Fortunately, today this is changing. (See Foundations of Family-Centered *Taharah*.)

Contemporary *chevrot* can take many forms. Some are synagogue volunteer committees. Others are community-wide volunteer organizations. Some exist as a combination of these. Still other communities are served by paid *taharah* professionals.

In addition to performing *taharah*, modern *chevrot*, also known as burial societies, may offer a wide variety of services across the spectrum of end-of-life care, reminiscent of their medieval counterparts and of the *landmanshaftn* so prevalent in immigrant communities in early America. Members may visit the sick, counsel and comfort families, vigil with the dying and the dead (known as being a *shomer*, or guard), and officiate at funerals and *shiva minyanim* (home prayer services). Some own cemeteries, and perform fundraising to help bury the poor; some offer public speaking about *taharah* as part of an outreach effort to educate the Jewish public about our death customs.

Chevrah kadisha members usually receive training as part of their orientation to the group's work. However, when the call comes in and trained personnel are not available, the novice team member may learn from other members, books, and from their own direct experience.

Foundations of Family-Centered *Taharah*

The idea of taking care of the dead in their own home is not new. Until the modern era, *taharah* took place in the parlor or front room of a family's home, with the family either participating or nearby as the *chevrah kadisha* performed its task.

According to Yaffa Eliach, writing about the 900-year history of Eishyshok, a Polish Jewish ghetto destroyed in the Holocaust:

> Until Eishyshok's final days [in the 1940s], most people died in their own homes, surrounded by their family. Immediately upon death, the family notified the *chevrah kadisha* and the *kvoresman* [grave digger].... The *kvoresman* would arrive at the house of the deceased carrying the *taharah* bret, the board on which bodies are laid for cleansing before burial; he then returned to the cemetery to dig the grave, leaving the actual purification of the body to the burial society, whose members arrived at the house soon afterward.[8]

Family-centered *taharah* draws on this idea of a past time when the family was part of the ritual.

It also draws on a do-it-yourself, anti-authority sentiment that evolved into the Counterculture Movement of the 1960s. An American public appalled by the Vietnam War came to reject authority in all its traditional forms. This led to activism and grand-scale changes in the American social landscape, including civil rights for blacks, feminism, gay rights, environmentalism, and a personalized approach to religious experience.

Issues around illness and death received the same sort of shake-up. Following such groundbreaking revelations as 1963's, *The American Way of Death*, by "muckraking" journalist Jessica Mitford, regulations were enacted to protect families from unscrupulous practices in the funeral industry. Many began to eschew the mechanization and formality of hospitals and funeral homes, shifting toward more

---

[8] Eliach, Yaffa. *There Once Was a World – A 900-year Chronicle of the Shtetl of Eishyshok*, Little Brown & Co., 1998. Page 246.

personalized, hands-on approaches. This resulted, among other things, in the development of the hospice and home funeral movements.

Hospice allows terminally ill patients to die peacefully at home, surrounded by their loved ones, with medical care focused on their comfort, rather than on "rescuing" them in a sterile, physician-centric hospital environment. Home hospice became a real option for all Americans when Congress made it a federally funded part of Medicare in 1982.[9] By 2011, about 45 percent of all U.S. deaths were under the care of a hospice program.[10]

Home funerals challenge the American funeral industry's rigid, somber approach, and the high cost and environmental unfriendliness of many of the standard practices.

Statistics on the frequency of home funerals are not readily available, but the National Home Funeral Alliance reports that it has about 220 home funeral guide members. Many have been trained in assisting families to prepare and honor their own dead by such organizations as Final Passages in Sebastopol, Calif., founded by Jerrigrace Lyons; Beyond Hospice, an on-line training founded by Donna Belk of Austin, Texas; and Crossings: Caring for Our Own at Death, founded by Elizabeth Knox of Takoma Park, Maryland.

Home funeral activists say that they want to help the public rethink death, and return it to the natural, profound and private event it once was. They are able to perform their home rituals because of laws on the books that allow U.S. families to keep their loved ones at home with them for up to three days following death. Professional supervision of a home funeral via a contracted funeral director is mandated in only eight U.S. states.[11]

---

[9] As part of the The Tax Equity and Fiscal Responsibility Act of 1982. From the article "Hospice: An HAA/NAHC Historical Perspective" (http://www.nahc.org/haa/history/)

[10] From the National Hospice and Palliative Care Organization's annual report, *NHPCO's Facts and Figures 2012: Hospice Care in America*. This figure does not appear in subsequent editions.

[11] Namely, Nebraska, New York, New Jersey, Indiana, Michigan, Louisiana,

To quote Lee Webster, vice president of the National Home Funeral Alliance and a home funeral guide:

> People who want home funerals don't want strangers doing everything for them. They want to take responsibility for themselves. They may want to design services and hold them in places of personal meaning, or transport their loved one in the family's truck, or simply stay by their side longer than usual. They don't fit into any package deal. They don't want cookie cutter services in parlors or slumber rooms or for-rent chapels. They don't want everything to be made easy. They want to work through their grief by participating in the process, by helping one another in practical ways, to feel it and keep going anyway.
>
> [Family-centered after-death care is a] conduit for clarity and shared experience at the deepest level — at a time when we are as close to mortality and mystery as humans can possibly fathom. ... Home funerals give families a choice and are empowering. ... Some families participate in the preparations as part of working through their grief. Giving people jobs to do is healing and creates connection.[12]

The Jewish funeral industry saw a parallel challenge to its authority, mostly focused on how the era's increasingly elaborate funerals ran counter to the Jewish tradition's more modest approach, as addressed in the book, *A Plain Pine Box*, by Rabbi Arnold M. Goodman, published in 1976. This lead to a revival of interest in *chevrah kadisha* and *taharah* for Jews of all backgrounds, which today has spawned the creation of dozens of *chevrot* across North America, and the international advocacy and training organization *Kavod v'Nichum*.

Family-centered *taharah* and *taharah*-like rituals are a natural outgrowth of the same sentiments that led to development of home funerals. No one is offering trainings in this field, or keeping records

---

Connecticut, and Illinois. This issue is discussed at length in *Restoring Families' Right to Choose: The call for funeral legislation change in America*, a statement issued by the National Home Funeral Alliance and available at http://www.homefuneralalliance.org.

[12] From an interview with Webster appearing on http://www.I'mSorrytoHear.com, a funeral planning Website.

about them. But indications are that, among liberal Jewish clergy, they may be relatively common, especially among rabbis who serve on *chevrot kadisha*.[13]

---

[13] An online posting by Avivah on two listserves for Jewish clergy on January 1, 2015, requesting examples of *taharah*-like rituals, yielded essays from ten rabbis and chaplains from across the U.S.; some even included their original liturgy. She is also personally aware of another ten or so who have told her about ceremonies they have conducted, or have written about online. Worthy of note: All of these examples involved women *roshes*. This may suggest a link between the arrival of family-centered *taharah* and the growing number of women in the fields of Jewish chaplaincy, the rabbinate, and other death care services.

Taharah Manuals, Ancient and Modern

As mentioned above, Berechiah's *Ma'avor Yabok* continues to provide the structural core of most *taharah* ritual manuals in use today. It consists of a collection of text citations culled from the *Tanach* and the rabbinic teachings known as the *Mishna*, plus original contributions from its author.

Texts excerpted in it were carefully chosen and placed with great care, to suggest additional layers of meaning. According to Kelman and Fendel:

> Just as with our regular prayer liturgy, when texts are extracted from their original position (that is, taken out of the *old* context and placed into a *new* context), there is a presumed intent on the part of the editor to make a specific point by selecting that excerpt. When this is done successfully, the classical text then functions as a powerful liturgical text, with the compiled verses often conveying ideas distinct from what was in their original context, yet also conjuring up that context. Collectively, these texts – both the composed texts and the excerpted classical texts – form a symphony of words and ideas leading to an orchestrated rite.[14]

Most modern *taharah* manuals include the same basic liturgy, but may vary in the form and local customs from which they draw. Still, they all strive for common ends.

Their content is designed to set proper intentions and include three entities in the conversation: God, the soul of the deceased, and the *taharah* team members in the room. They are based on Kabbalistic ideas that support the transition of the soul of the deceased, and specifically honor and guide the soul, which is considered to be present in the *taharah* room.

Conventional *taharah* manuals include a minimum of five specific ritual actions and associated liturgy, namely: (1) preliminary prayers and setting intentions; (2) physically washing and cleaning the

---

[14] Kelman, Stuart, and Fendel, Dan. *Chesed Shel Emet, The Truest Act of Kindness.* 3rd Edition, Berkeley, CA: EKS Publishing, 2013. Page 6.

deceased; (3) spiritually "purifying" the body and soul of the deceased by pouring water (or submersing the body) to simulate a *mikvah*; (4) dressing the deceased in *tachrichim* and a wrapping sheet (*sovev*) and placing them into the casket (some cemeteries allow shroud-only burial); and (5) concluding prayers.

In recent times many manuals have added three more non-ritual actions: a team briefing before the ritual; tidying up the *taharah* room and reorganizing supplies when finished; and a team debriefing after the ritual.

In addition, manuals guide the team in appropriate actions that preserve the dignity and modesty of the deceased while preparing the body for burial. These actions treat all Jews the same, no matter their status in life. Most manuals also include variations specific to the local community, so it is natural to see local variations in the liturgy. (See the bibliography for examples of modern traditional *taharah* manuals.)

Classic *Taharah*

The classic approach to *taharah*, as we have defined it, operates under the foundational assumption that the soul of the deceased (*neshamah*) is present in the room, and that it is not only comforted, but also assisted in its transition to the next world by the *taharah* ritual. It is this commitment to the soul's post-mortem needs that guides the team to show utmost respect to the soul and to its body, the holy vessel used in life, and thus, to put those needs first and foremost.

What does a soul need to help it move from this world to the next, from *olam hazeh* to *olam habah*? For an answer, we turn to the deep and robust body of wisdom inherent in our traditions. This approach has been the preferred one for Jews for centuries, and remains so today. For observant families it is a natural fit, but even Jewish families that rarely think about their faith, turn to the comfort of tradition and the trusted, long-standing approach of their community *chevrah* when death occurs.

The *taharah* ritual includes specific liturgy, along with specific actions, and as we have noted, this combination appears to work. It has lasted in its current form for some 400-plus years, and we don't know how long it was around prior to being written down. Traditions don't just survive, century after century, for no reason. They persist because they respond to a continuing need, and effectively achieve their objectives. Over time, the health of the Jewish community has been supported in part by its adherence to these well-established methods of handling and honoring death. We continue this tradition today, promoting that which has worked for generations to honor and respect both the holy souls and holy bodies of our dead.

Classic *taharah* rituals are performed by *chevrah kadisha* teams whose observance and style can vary significantly from one community to another. Some teams (and their *roshim*) are very strict in how they implement this holy ritual, while others feel that augmenting the beauty and grace of the rite can enhance *kavanah*. They may include music, for example, such as by chanting the liturgy, or inviting participants to hum *niggunim* (wordless melodies) during their work. Some share chants derived from the Hebrew liturgy, such as those developed for this purpose by Rabbi Shefa Gold.[15]

---

[15] See both of the following references in the bibliography for her chants: *To Midwife a Soul* by Richard A. Light, and *The Magic of Hebrew Chant: Healing the Spirit, Transforming the Mind, Deepening Love*, by Rabbi Shefa Gold.

Traditional Motivations

Why do people seek out classic *taharah*? Rick offers the following experience, of when he was first introduced to this work:

> There I was, at 46-years-old, lying on the table, dead. Six intensely focused people were huddled around me reciting specific liturgy from Scripture and dressing me in burial shrouds. Not knowing how to be dead, I tried to just be "dead weight," loose, relaxed, and present. As I followed their progress, I soon found myself in a bright white light. I was gone. All that existed for me was the light. That's all I could see, hear, feel, experience. Time stopped. Place stopped. Voices stopped. Life stopped. I was suspended in pure, brilliant "beingness;" aware, but not limited in time, space or personality.
>
> Earlier that week in the Spring of 1996, a friend of mine who was our "lay rabbi" at the local *shul* (synagogue), had called me, suggesting that I attend a training in a nearby city about an "esoteric side of Judaism that we should check out to see if we want to do it here." He had asked me to go, since I was the only Jew he knew who was into "weird spiritual things." It turned out to be training for the *chevrah kadisha,* the Jewish team whose job it is to prepare the dead for burial. We had a verbal training in the morning. Now, we were doing a role-play experiential training in which the team practiced the entire procedure of the *taharah,* the ritual of washing and dressing the dead. Luckily, this time they were simulating the washing of the body and the spiritual pouring of water. I was, after all, not really dead.
>
> Suddenly, I was "awakened" by one of the team. I slowly opened my eyes and tried to adjust to the real world again. They said, "We could tell by the look on your face that you were somewhere else!" Where I went and what happened to me are still unexplained phenomena. When I explained what had happened, everyone was amazed, including me. It was an extraordinary experience for all of us; so much so that I returned home to start a local *chevrah kadisha*. If a dry run could be so transformative, how much more powerful must be the real thing![16]

---

[16] Light, Richard A., *Rites of Death, The Beauty and Power of Jewish Tradition.* Santa Fe, NM: Terra Nova Press, 2015. Pages 48-49.

The power of traditional liturgy is evident in this experience. It is not something easily explainable, nor quantifiable. There is simply a profound reason why this approach has survived the ages. And today, communities continue to create *chevrot kadisha* to support their needs.

Most Jews don't focus much on Jewish death rituals, funeral procedures, or mortuary options. Jewish life in general is about living. However, the lifecycle calendar of Jewish tradition includes death right there next to birth, *brit milah*, marriage, and other community and family celebrations. When death happens, families turn to their tradition: the trusted, long-standing wisdom of the Torah and sages, along with the local community's historical customs for preparing the body, mourning the loss, and surviving in the midst of tragedy.

This time-tested *taharah* ritual is here today in its current form not because it is flashy or fashionable, but because devoted *chevrah* members have maintained it intact, and because generations of Jewish families have experienced it as effective, both in meeting needs in this world and, they believe, otherworldly ends as well. Faced with the unknowns of death, we trust the classic *taharah* to usher the soul on its journey while providing comfort to families who want their loved one taken care of in a trusted manner.

The Role of the Traditional *Rosh*

The *rosh* is the leader of the *taharah* ritual. This person is responsible for everything that happens in the *taharah* room, as well as what takes place before and after the ritual itself.

The job of the *rosh* typically includes a number of logistical and managerial duties. These may include communicating with funeral home personnel; calling together a suitable team; briefing and preparing the team prior to the ritual; assigning tasks; guiding participants and making decisions during the ritual to ensure a smooth flow of work; chairing the debriefing afterwards; noting the status of *taharah* supplies; and overseeing the cleaning of the room after the *taharah* is completed.

After arranging for the *taharah*, the *rosh* usually arrives at the funeral home prior to the rest of the team, ready to determine the state of affairs. Where is the *meit*? What is the condition of the body and was there an obvious cause of death? Are there health hazards for the *chevrah* members and are there medical devices that will need to be removed or handled? Are adequate supplies at hand and is the *taharah* room clean and ready? Are there funeral home personnel available to help if something goes awry during the procedure?[17] Has the *taharah* team been provided the *meit*'s Hebrew name and prayer shawl (*tallit*) for use during the ceremony, and guidance as to what to do with jewelry and other personal property found on the *meit*?

With this information, the *rosh* will be able to ascertain which aspects of the ritual it will be possible to complete, and which the team will have to forgo. Each situation is different, and the *rosh* is the person who decides how it will unfold.

If, for example, the body is mangled or badly decomposed, it may be impossible to wash and dress it. To attempt to do so would not

---

[17] For example, if the casket lid does not fit properly, the *meit*'s size prevents them from fitting into a casket or the team from lifting them, or if the water and drainage in the room do not work properly.

show the *meit* proper *kavod*. Some *roshim* do not attempt a ritual, considering this situation an "unworkable" *taharah*, and an additional tragedy for the *meit*. Others, however, are open to creative alternatives. Under such conditions, these teams feel that if they hold the sacred intention of *kavod hameit*, the *taharah* goals can still be accomplished. An approach often taken is to place the *meit* into the *aron* (casket), lay the *tachrichim* over the body bag, read some meaningful passages, and consider the rite complete.

Traditional *Taharah* Boundaries

A major principal of classic *taharah* is that it is performed so as to foster a sense of Jewish community and connection among everyone involved: the dying and their families and friends, their synagogue family, the ritual's participants, the Jewish community at large, and those who have gone before us.

The image of the enduring, ever-consistent *taharah* ritual ties into the idea of Jewish continuity. Changes to the ritual may be rejected by some *roshim* simply because the tradition is strong, and to interrupt it would represent a break in this holy chain.

Taharah is performed by Jews for Jews, thus inviting participants to experience a deep connection to their Jewish spiritual and communal heritage and identity. Conversely, non-Jews are generally not involved with the performance of the rite, and do not receive *taharah* after death. Because of this, most teams have policies to resolve boundary issues, such as how the Judaism of participants will be determined, and what non-Jews who wish to be involved can and cannot do.

Some traditional teams are open to performing *taharah* for any Jew, by any definition, under any circumstances. In some cases, some *chevrot* decline to perform *taharah* rituals, even for Orthodox Jews. Others leave it up to the leader, or to individual members, as to the conditions under which they are willing to participate.

The most common situation in which a *taharah* is declined by some teams is when the *meit* will be cremated or embalmed. Some teams, when faced with a *meit* who died violently, believe we should "show Heaven our shock" by not cleaning the body, and burying it with all evidence intact.

Boundaries and policies are unique to each community, and may even vary within communities. Some *roshim* decline requests to place mementos in the casket with the deceased. They may not allow chanting or singing in the *taharah* room, instead expecting silence to prevail throughout the ceremony. And they may consider it compulsory to help the decedent fall within traditional parameters, such as to perform ritual circumcision on an uncircumcised *meit*, or decline to place *tallit* or *kippah* on a Jewish woman for whom this has been requested.

Some may encourage families to override the wishes of the deceased if these include cremation, advocating for burying their loved one instead. Jewish teachings hold that cremation creates a permanent, irreparable separation between body and soul, blocking a loved one's ability to return to Earth with the future coming of the Messiah. For some Jews, this is seen as a catastrophe worth preempting.

Some teams may encourage families to expedite the funeral, even if this means holding it before all out-of-town relatives can arrive. And when faced with questions about the physical sex of the *meit*, most *chevrot* follow the custom that the *taharah* team is assigned so as to match the decedent's birth gender. (For example, a *meit* who considered herself a woman, but was born with male genitalia, would be washed by men, even if this would not have been her preference.[18])

Most *chevrot* do not allow family members to participate in a *taharah*. Some do allow it, or allow it only on a limited basis such as by inviting them into the room near the end to tie the last knot on the *tachrichim*. Often teams say that they chose this approach for their organization after an experience in which family members attended a *taharah* and turned out to be emotionally unable to handle the procedure, or spoke or acted judgmentally toward the team while in the *taharah* room, to the point that *chevra* members felt distracted and unable to perform their tasks with *kavanah*.

It is important to remember that all of these policies are specific to each local *chevrah* and vary widely across the spectrum of communities.

---

[18] We call this being transgender, an occurance that was famliar to our ancient rabbis. For more on this see: Dzmura, Noach (Editor). *Balancing on the Mechitza: Transgender in Jewish Community*. Berkeley, CA: North Atlantic Books, 2010.

In a nutshell, for classic *taharah*, traditional, liturgical-based procedures trump personal preference, as long as the family and deceased are shown appropriate respect and dignity in the view of the ritual team and *rosh*.

Family-Centered Jewish Washing Ceremonies

Part of Judaism's capacity to survive and thrive over the millennia has been its ability to adapt to fit changing times and needs. This openness to change has helped ensure that Jewish values live on, now and into the future.

As mentioned above, some of Judaism's more esoteric elements went "out of style" for several generations. Today that is changing, as Jews reach out for meaningful ritual and discover that practices such as *taharah* are not only available, but can be modified to serve their own circumstances and wishes.

A family-centered washing ritual can be a matter of improvisation on the part of the coordinator, who can be called by the traditional title of *rosh*, or by the home funeral industry's preferred title, guide. The ceremony may or may not use trained participants, a traditional manual, or any given particular element of the more familiar *taharah* ritual.

The ritual can be conducted wherever it would be most appropriate and satisfactory for the family. Equipment considerations will come into play if they want the "full amount" of water used; otherwise the location is more flexible.

The team can include trained volunteers, and may be all of the same sex as the decedent, and may be Jews. But it could just as likely be made up of family members, friends, nurses and aides, funeral directors, clergy and others, of varied genders and religions. (More about this in the Modesty Issues section of the chapter Family-Centered Ceremony Boundaries.)

The *rosh* may prepare the participants at a pre-briefing meeting and assign tasks, or this may come together at the time of the ritual. The leader guides participants during the ritual, monitoring the team members' wishes, level of comfort and understanding to determine if modifications are needed. Debriefing afterwards is another ideal that may or may not occur.

A family-centered ceremony may or may not follow the traditional liturgy. Classic elements are offered as options for the family to consider at each step of the ritual, using a *Ma'avor Yabok*-based manual as the starting place (much like traditional *taharah*).

Goals for the liturgy are the same as in the traditional approach, including setting intentions, honoring and guiding the *neshamah*, and directing the *taharah* team. Sections can be the same as a traditional *taharah* as well.

But the liturgy can just as well become a springboard to creating a ritual that fully satisfies a given family, filled with song, poetry, art and more, while meeting specific family needs such as to reduce or eliminate water, to dress the *meit* in street clothing, or to follow the ceremony with cremation.

By making such rituals available, Jewish washing ceremony guides enable families who might never otherwise experience *taharah* to gain its benefits: comfort for themselves and honor for their loved one.

Family-Centered Motivations

Families that choose a family-centered washing ceremony may be motivated by traditional thoughts regarding the soul – the idea that without specific prayers and rituals performed in specific ways, the soul will not move on to God in peace.

But often, their inspirations are less theological and more about personal expressions of love and spirituality. Some have been inspired along this path by stories about *taharah* experiences that were not ideal. For example, a friend who was deeply hurt by the decision of a strict *taharah rosh* to not permit family members into the washing room, or to allow them in but refuse to let them speak or touch the deceased.

The following include a number of the reasons we have heard:

Our loved one was connected to Judaism, so a taharah *would have been meaningful for him, but as artists we feel the traditional approach would not be sufficiently beautiful or spiritually expressive for us.*

Our loved one was not religious and chose to be cremated. We do not wish to override her wishes, but we are connected to Judaism and feel pain due to her choice. A home taharah *would be a great compromise.*

We want a way to demonstrate our love and devotion to our loved one, who has died in our arms, and we can't bear to let him go. Washing and blessing him would be a meaningful way to ease his departure from our lives.

Our loved one never left her home without her clothing and hair just so; being able to wash and dress her, accompanied by prayers, would allow us to show the ultimate respect to the woman that she was.

Our loved one would not qualify for a traditional taharah, *because he will be cremated (or never formally converted to Judaism, etc.). But we still want him to have one.*

We are concerned that an Orthodox taharah *would bring dishonor to our loved one. (He lived as an uncircumcised Jewish man, and to circumcise him now would be to disfigure him. Or, she considered herself a woman, but was born a man. To have her washed by men would be immodest, we feel.).*

In other words, the reasons can be as varied as the families that request a family-centered *taharah*. What they all have in common is their devotion to their loved one, and a commitment to "do everything they can for them," as they understand it. This is done either by participating in the ritual, or by making sure a ceremony is held in their loved one's honor that accommodates their wishes.

Variation among home *taharah* ceremonies simply need not be a concern. Each one will be quite unique, and yet completely authentic, in that its *rosh* has provided some degree of customary content and respectfully honored Jewish boundaries (more on boundaries in the *Halachah* and *Taharah* section, below).

Family-centered ceremonies can be seen as a return to the way things were done in the distant past, before standardized liturgy and mortuary formality pointed practitioners in the direction of fixed approaches. Providers of family-centered *taharah* feel that this form of ritual meets the same goals as the traditional model, while accommodating the needs of modern families, the contemporary world, and Judaism today, and that it is a perfect fit for the growing hospice model of death with dignity at home.

Halachah and *Taharah*

Some in the Jewish community consider classic *taharah* the "kosher" way – the "only" way that this ritual may be performed. We take inspiration from these individuals, who are devoted to the sanctity and continuity of this craft, and do not mean to suggest that they are not correct.

We would, however, like to point out four things. First, the *taharah* liturgy was most likely free form from the times of the early Hebrews until the 1600's, when *Ma'avar Yabok* was codified. Second, home *taharot* would have been common until the rise of funeral homes in the 1800's. Third, family-centered and home-based *taharot* are seeing growing interest among Jews of all backgrounds today. And fourth, the terms "*halachic*" and "kosher" cannot actually be applied here. Little among the elements of a traditional *taharah* is, in fact, *halachic*, meaning fixed by mandate of Jewish law (*halachah*). Rather, it is a collection of customs handed down over time, that has changed through the ages and will continue to change, depending on many factors.

Rabbi Mosha Epstein, author of what is considered the *halachic* standard for this rite, has this to say:

> ... Much of taharah procedure is custom, rather than halacha. Inevitably, questions arise concerning which customs to adopt. Chevros kadisha adopt practices which they believe will best honor and prepare the deceased to meet the Master of the Universe in the purest possible state. ... Some of the customs adopted are dictated by the realities and resources available in our community. ... The customs we adopted are in no way binding on others, and may evolve here as well, depending on future experience, need and resources.[19]

In his book, Rabbi Epstein sets out various *halachic* positions on

---

[19] Epstein, Mosha. *Taharah Manual of Practices, Including Halacha Decisions of Hagaon Harav Moshe Feinstein, zt'l.* Bridgeport, CT: 1995. From the introduction. (Note that *chevros* and *chevrot* are different pronunciations of the same Hebrew word.)

aspects of the *taharah* ritual. The rabbinic decisors (*poskim*) he quotes agree on only a few points (as is usual when a group of Jewish scholars discuss anything!), namely: that *taharah* is mandatory for all Jews; that the dead must be dressed in Jewish burial shrouds; that the ritual involves water; and that those who provide *taharah* should be pure themselves, namely "kosher, outstanding and honored members of the Jewish community."

All the fine points of the ritual, from what the *tachrichim* should look like and how much water must be used to what should be said and done during the ceremony, are a matter of local practice and the decisions of the *rosh*. And beyond that, even when minimal standards cannot be met, exceptions are permitted. Epstein allows that (we paraphrase):

There are *poskim* that permit families to decline *taharah* or shrouds. While some say rabbis must insist on *taharah* and *tachrichim*; others say it is good to instruct families, but not argue with them.

There are *poskim* that allow, or even recommend, modification of the ritual. If the *meit* was not religious, for example, some *poskim* say that the central words of the ritual, "*tahor hu/taharah hi*" (he is pure, she is pure), should be omitted. Other *poskim* say to provide the full ritual, no matter what.

There are *poskim* that permit *taharah* prior to cremation, a ruling that tangentially allows this "unthinkable" violation of Jewish law. Many say *taharah* should be refused in cases when cremation is planned, but some say it is permitted with cremation if the children arranged for it, but not if the *meit* did so.

There are *poskim* who mandate that providers of *taharah* be *tahor* themselves (i.e. ritually pure; that is, having gone to *mikvah* prior to the ritual), but this is becoming rare. Most *chevrot* today do not require *tahor* personal status, even for women. Some do prefer team members who honor *Shabbat*, or require a preponderance of *Shabbat* observant members on a team for an observant *meit*.

In fact, even non-Jews may perform a *taharah*, Epstein says. When necessary, such as when there are no Jews in the area, or so that a burial can take place on the second day of a holiday, all requirements for Jewish participants can be waived. Some say, if there is only one Jew available to participate, that person should be the one to fetch and pour the water, and understand and say the prayers.

Many consider the amount of water used to purify the *meit* to be the defining factor of the *taharah*. But even here there is no universal criterion. The most commonly used standard derives from a Talmudic discourse about what is needed to purify a man who has had a seminal emission. He can use a mikvah, or, he can pour nine *kavim* of water on himself.

> "The rabbis ordained that after any seminal discharge, whether or not resulting from copulation, total immersion is required in order to be ritually pure again for prayer or study of the Torah. Since this was a rabbinical institution, immersion in drawn water or pouring nine *kav* ... of water over the body was considered sufficient. (BK 82a, b)[20]

So exactly how big is a *kav*? According to the Talmud, it is equal to 24 *beitzim* (eggs). So how many ounces were there in a chicken's egg 2,000 years ago? We can only guess, and interpretations vary widely. Most *chevrot* follow the understanding that nine *kavim* is between 4.5 and 6 gallons, or 24 quarts of water. But Rav Epstein writes that his *chevrah* uses 5 gallons and permits 3.5 gallons (14 quarts) if it is enough to thoroughly wet the *meit*.

The bottom line, according to Rav Epstein, is to honor the dead, and to apply common sense: to "do unto the *meit* as you would want to be treated" yourself. There must be *kavanah*, and there must be good intentions. That's really it. "We do the best we can," is the motto for most *chevrot*.

The mandate for water, for example, can only be fulfilled when water is available. When there is no water, the *chevrah* can still satisfy the mandate to "do they best we can" by saying some prayers and

---

[20] Jewish Virtual Library (http://www.jewishvirtuallibrary.org/jsource/judaica/ejud_0002_0001_0_00161.html)

treating the *meit* with utmost kindness. Is this still a *taharah*? There may be some disagreement, but we would say, yes, it is.

What is important is the holiness of this work, the attitudes of those involved, and the intention to honor and respect the deceased and those left behind. Indeed, there has always been room for accommodation, as there must be in something so specific, and so enduring, as *taharah*. To follow in the rhythm of these elements, by some means and with an open heart, can, by our understanding, be understood to be a "full" and "complete" *taharah* and an honorable sending off of a loved one to the Holy One of Blessing.

The Role of the Family-Centered *Rosh*

A family-centered Jewish washing ceremony can be coordinated by a rabbi or Jewish hospice chaplain, a Jewish hospice employee or a licensed funeral director who works in private homes, a member of the local *chevrah kadisha* or synagogue Caring Community, or any family member or member of the community with the necessary knowledge and skills.

Perhaps the most important skills are ritual continuity and containment, the ability to keep a group of people focused on a ceremony, and to bring back this focus if it gets interrupted. Most liberal rabbis and Jewish chaplains today have extensive experience with this art form.

For a *rosh* with this ability, distractions such as distressed family members are not a reason to disavow allowing them into the *taharah* space. The distress is natural, and can be honored and accommodated. The mourners can choose to step outside the room when they become overwhelmed, or withdraw from participation, at any time. The team may choose to shift from completing the ritual to comforting the mourner. Since there is no mandate beyond custom that the ceremonial elements of the ritual be completed, what has already been completed can be enough. Whatever needs to be done can be done.

Like traditional leaders, the family-centered *rosh* has many tasks. They also handle communications with the funeral home; but they may also work with the patient's hospice team, or be on it. They must obtain permission to perform the ritual from all relevant decision makers, such as the next of kin (or agreement among these if there are several); the healthcare proxy (Durable Power of Attorney for Healthcare); the estate manager (Financial Power of Attorney), and others.

They convene a team to perform the ritual, and if the family will be participating, they will need to train, orient and continually counsel them. Guides should always set out a rule before the ritual starts, and gain buy-in, that they are the sole arbiter of questions during the ritual, because no arguments are permitted once it is under way. Participants will also need to expect a debriefing afterwards, to ensure their emotional health.

Roshim may be responsible for providing the *taharah* supplies, including the cleaning supplies, linens, *tachrichim* and other ritual items. They may also be responsible for creating a space in which the ritual will be held, providing tables, lighting, fans or heaters, and equipment to facilitate the pouring of water, such as a slant board (so that the ceremony can be held in a shower), a portable tub (on a bed), or an enclosed canopy tent (in the family's yard).

Family-Centered Ceremony Boundaries

After ritual containment, a second and equally important skill for the family-centered *rosh* is to be able to "follow their intuition." They need to know where the boundaries lie, for themselves, for common decency and *kavod hameit*, for Judaism, and for the laws of their community, etc. They want to be open to accommodating family requests, but it is solely on their shoulders to vigilantly maintain the limits of what will be allowed.

The following list suggests potential issues around the ritual where a family may request accommodation. It appears here in order to invite you, the reader, to check in with yourself and develop a sense of your own limits. What could you ride out, and where would you have to draw the line if you were the *rosh*?

The family-centered guide's top priority always remains to accommodate the family while providing respect to the *meit*. If a family's request exceeds your capacity to support it, your sense of what's "OK," then you always have options (and telling the family outright that they are *wrong* is not one of them[21]).

You can try to talk them out of it, explaining that you cannot support it for the reasons you have, and see if they will back off and conform with your approach. You can turn the ritual over to them for the duration of the request, explaining that you will need to step out of the picture temporarily. Or you can find them someone else to step in and fulfill this part of their plan.

✡ Religion of the *Meit*

The *rosh* may be open to performing a *taharah* for a decedent or family that is not Jewish. They may feel this is OK as long as even one person involved in the case has a sincere connection to Jewish

---

[21] Of course, if what they suggest breaks the law or would offend common decency, outright disagreement is your only option. We are talking about cases that fall short of this standard.

life and practice. It is for the comfort and honor of this Jew that the ritual would be performed.

If the decedent considered themselves Jewish, whether or not they had Jewish parents or a conversion, the *rosh* may be open to performing the full classic ritual, or prefer a modified one.

A *rosh* who cannot in good conscience perform a traditional *taharah* on a non-Jew (even if they loved Judaism) may be open to a modified version, altering the words or gestures to keep it within the bounds of their own sensibility. Or they may want to turn the ritual over to someone else, so that the family's wishes remain respected.

A liturgy like that found in *Final Kindness* (see bibliography), all in English and without Jewish-specific teachings, is appropriate for any non-Jew who was part of the Jewish community. When performing a *Final Kindness* ritual, it would not be appropriate to use symbols reserved for demarcating Jewish dead, such as a Star of David on the casket; Jewish burial garments, a prayer shawl and *kippah* (skull cap); and the anointing elements used by some *chevrot* including holy earth from Israel, pottery shards, and vinegar and egg.

If the decedent did not consider themselves part of the Jewish community, however, we believe that a *rosh* should draw a sharp line, out of respect for the tradition and those who practice it. It would *not* be appropriate to use Hebrew prayer or Jewish theology in preparing this decedent. In fact, some *roshim* may feel that it is more appropriate for non-Jews to prepare this deceased for their final journey.

✡ Religion of Participants

If non-Jewish members of the decedent's circle of care ask to participate in the ritual, the guide will need to clarify, in their own heart, what traditional priorities they will need to see satisfied, and how they will achieve this.

Which elements of the ritual will be shared among all participants and which will be assigned only to Jews? Will the *rosh* make this decision known, or keep it private? The answers will come down to the guide's own sense of what or whom to exclude, so as to maintain the standards of their heart, weighed against the possibility that acting on this may offend members of the group and disrupt the warm, harmonious atmosphere they are wanting to foster.

Ensuring the group's *kavanah* is a high priority for the *rosh*. They may therefore choose to exclude non-Jews from participating in the recitation of prayers, feeling that only someone who understands them, or to whom they apply, should take on this role.

In the same way, a *rosh* may feel that it is more appropriate for Jews to pour the *taharah* water for spiritual purification of the meit, or they may ask only the more ritually observant participants to fill, carry and pour the ablution buckets.

The *rosh* may hold to a standard for keeping the *meit* accompanied at all times. If so, they may choose to reserve the role of designated *shomer* for Jews, or for family members.

✡ Modesty Issues

Unlike classic *taharah* teams, the family-centered team can be composed of people of different sexes. Since one of the priorities of *taharah* is to maintain the modesty of the deceased and the appropriate comportment of the team, this may be a challenge.

For the *rosh*, this starts with being very careful to choose appropriate ritual participants. The guide should personally interview and screen each candidate prior to the ritual, going to some lengths to explain the gravity of the project and to ascertain their capacity to handle it. This is an experience that can be lengthy, somber, physically strenuous, emotionally intense and potentially shocking. The *rosh* may want to ask the candidate exactly the nature of their relationship with the decedent, and if they have ever been around a dead body before.

The sexes of the participants and deceased, by birth, identity, or surgical or hormonal modification, need not necessarily be guiding factors when deciding whom to include or rule out. What matters is who would be appropriate to be around the decedent in a state of undress and vulnerability. A spouse or partner is a logical choice for a participant, if they wish, as is anyone who has been providing personal care to the decedent in their decline, such as toileting and bathing.

The opinion of family members about the sexual identity of the *meit* may also be an issue:

> What matters is how the *meit* saw themselves, and from there, who the *meit* would have been comfortable with.... The "appropriateness" aspect can be touchy, as a family member might have seen the *meit* as one gender and make a decision based on that, when the *meit* saw themselves as a different gender.[22]

Others who wish to participate, but for whom seeing the decedent's intimate areas would be inappropriate, can be permitted, asking them to step outside the room, or to turn and face away during certain parts of the ritual.

✡ Non-Traditional Practices

The dying person and family may wish to accompany their ceremony with decisions that fall outside of Jewish tradition. The family-centered *rosh* should be ready to hear this in most every case they handle. Plans can include such things as cremation, having no funeral, holding a public viewing, donating the body to science, or even physician-assisted suicide.

For families who will not otherwise be having a Jewish funeral, or a funeral at all (such as when cremation and scattering or distribution of ashes is planned), the Jewish washing ceremony can serve this purpose, bringing Jewish community and connection to this family and the deceased.

---

[22] From a private e-mail conversation with Dr. Joel L. Kushner, director of the Institute for Judaism, Sexual Orientation and Gender Identity at Hebrew Union College, Jewish Institute of Religion, and a board member of the Jewish Burial Society of Southern California.

The *rosh* may be open to having the ceremony cut short so that the *meit* can be readied for a family-requested viewing, allowing for preparations such as cosmetics, hairdressing, and the embalming technique known as facial feature setting.[23]

The guide may be open to a family request to delay the funeral until family members can arrive from out of town. Because of modern refrigeration or the appropriate use of ice packs, a *taharah* can take place even a week or two after death without significant complications.

In cases where cremation occurs immediately after death, with a service scheduled afterwards, the custom of providing *shomrim* for the deceased can still be observed until the funeral or memorial service, with a *shomer* or guide focusing their *kavanah* on the urn.

A family-centered *rosh* may feel that the circumstances of the decedent's case are irrelevant to the determination of what should be arranged. Being unable to complete the ritual in the traditional sense may not be a concern, based on the sentiment that, whatever can be done with the current team can be enough.

✡ A Pretty Picture

Holding the ceremony in their private space, a family may choose to modify the traditional ritual, creating one that is more to their taste and sensibilities.

They may wish to introduce artistic touches, a Jewish custom known as *hiddur mitzvah*. The *rosh* may permit, or even suggest, such elements as music (singing or instrumental); scents (perfumed candles, soaps, oils, water essences or sprigs of herbs); decorative flowers or pictures; and the use of electronics, such as playing or recording videos.

---

[23] Some mortuaries set the features of all *meitim* in their care, prior to the *taharah* ritual, and do not give the *taharah* team another option. It consists of locking shut the eyes and mouth by introduction of foreign objects.

Or, they may wish to drop basic elements of the traditional ceremony and procedure. Requests may include wanting to reduce or eliminate water, not touch the decedent, reject gloves and gowns for participants, use an all-English liturgy, replace *tachrichim* with street clothing, and more.

The point is that, even if the group performs the ritual with music and art, or without water, the ceremony can be experienced as being just as complete, even as "kosher" as a more traditional ritual, as long as the participants are comforted, and believe that the *neshamah* of the *meit* is experiencing it the same way.

Judaism, after all, has a long history of substituting an imaginary version of a sacred act for the act itself, holding that the *kavanah* is enough. After the destruction of the Holy Temple in Jerusalem (in the year 70) terminated all animal sacrifice, for example, the Rabbis of the Talmud chose to replace each of the scheduled offerings with similarly timed prayer services in which the sacrifices were described, but not conducted.

Thus, a family-centered *rosh* should carry the widest possible range of options in their back pocket, as it were, so as to find a ritual option that suits each family and circumstance when the time comes. Some families are best served with a straight-down-the-line, classic *taharah*. Some are not.

✡ Beyond Jewish Bounds

The above discussion should have helped to give a sense of the range of issues that may arise in a family-centered *taharah* ritual, which some may want to call a "Jewish washing ceremony" because it does not meet one or more of their requirements for a "proper" *taharah* by their own definition.

Now we consider the question, "When is a washing ritual not *Jewish*?" What sorts of things must be *excluded* from a ritual because they are "foreign practices," a concept underlined extensively in the Torah and very important to many Jews.

Avivah studied the question of the boundaries of Judaism vis a vis foreign practices for her rabbinic Master's thesis, which explored Jewish interest in yoga today, and the wish by some yoga teachers, including herself, to find appropriate ways to blend Jewish and Hindu elements in their classes.

The trend to mix Jewish and foreign practices, she found, arises from two U.S. cultural trends that began taking hold in the 1960s: New Age Spirituality, and the Jewish Renewal Movement founded by Rabbi Zalman Shachter-Shalomi. The New Age movement emphasizes the personal over the communal, and encourages individuals to study the practices of all the world's faiths, so as to choose for themselves those they find meaningful.

The downside of the New Age approach is syncretism, a blending of practices that undermines the integrity of their sources. Concern that Judaism is being corrupted and misused is the main reason that many Jews consider ideas such as "Jewish Yoga" jarring.

Avivah wrote:

> Finding the middle path between New Age syncretism and Jewish exclusivity ... is the express goal of this thesis and my work as a Jewish Yoga teacher.[24]

"And I might add," Avivah asserts today, "that this is the goal of my work as a family-centered *taharah roshah* as well."

Her thesis concluded that the absolute boundary between "Jewish" and "not" really depends on the individual considering the question and the community in which they function.

Halachah strongly proscribes the use of words and actions that, for the person using them (or for others looking on), there is an association with non-Jewish religious practice. Thus, to wrap a *meit* in a colourful silk Buddhist-style shroud, or to decorate the casket with paints and markers (as is popular at many non-Jewish home funerals), might be like blasphemy for some families, while others

---

[24] Erlick, Avivah W., *Breathing Life into Jewish Bones: How to deepen Jewish spirituality with Yoga-based contemplative movement*, an unpublished manuscript submitted in fulfilment of the requirements for the degree of Master's in Rabbinic Studies, Academy for Jewish Religion, California, 2009. p. 106.

would experience them only as a *hiddur mitzvah*.

The deciding factor, again, would be the sensibility of the *rosh*, in the context of the family, asking themselves if anyone in this family would be more offended than comforted by this choice.

A wake (putting a decedent on display) is an example of a practice that is clearly *not* Jewish for many, because of its strong association with traditions outside of Judaism. A lengthy gathering (traditionally three days) held with the dead person lying in state was historically part of Buddhist, Catholic and other rites, but only rarely in Judaism.

Jews do provide accompanying after death using a *shomer*, but the guard does not view the *meit*. Looking upon the face of a *meit* is considered impolite because they cannot look back. Rather, the *shomer* situates themselves near the *meit*, and seeks to comfort the *neshamah* of the *meit* by studying Psalms.

Prayers and gestures from religions other than Judaism can also be considered clearly beyond the bounds. To want to incorporate the "Our Father" prayer, or the swinging of a Catholic incense burner during a *taharah* suggests that this is not about the Jewish faith and the ancient chain of tradition that shapes it. We feel it would be more appropriate to follow a liturgy such as *Final Kindness* and leave out non-Jewish elements.

Or, if the family insists on having non-Jewish symbolic elements included, the *rosh* could ask the family to provide them, or reach out to a religious leader of the other faith and invite them to participate and offer these components, while the *rosh* steps outside the room.

In a nutshell: In family-centered *taharah*, preference trumps tradition, within the fixed boundaries of honor, respect, Jewish sensibilities, and giving comfort, as determined by the *rosh* in real time.

A Nice Jewish Question

How shall we, as Jews, show kindness and honor to our dead, support the soul of the deceased in transition, and at the same time, comfort and respect those who must carry on without them?

Today, Jews are answering this challenge in both classic and family-centered ways. These are Jews who love the Holy One and love their communities. They are expressing that love in different ways to show honor and respect to their dead.

But what makes a *taharah* a *taharah*?

Ultimately, you must answer this question for yourself.

We have discussed both ends of the spectrum of practices. We have shared the power, beauty and values that can shine through a *taharah* ritual, no matter how it is performed. For us, the holiness of the rite is the driving factor.

We feel that the bottom line standard for what qualifies as a *Jewish* ritual of washing the dead is that it be based in some way on the traditional liturgy, that its participants apply *kavanah* and best intention to the task, that kindness and respect are paramount, and that it excludes ritual elements that are explicitly non-Jewish.

Furthermore, we strongly feel that the central lesson of *taharah* for all of us is that we should learn from this ritual to treat others with respect, kindness, honor, and dignity while they are still alive.

About the Authors

Rabbi Avivah W. Erlick, BCC, is a rabbi and chaplain in private practice, and owns a clergy referral agency called LA Community Chaplaincy Services. Through her hospice work, she became interested in providing creative post-death ritual that is both authentically Jewish and family-centric. The result is Sacred Waters, possibly the world's first mobile *Tahara* service. Rabbi Avivah is a founding member of the Jewish Burial Society of Southern California. Ordained a transdenominational rabbi in 2009 by the Academy for Jewish Religion, Calif., she completed a hospital residency in interfaith chaplaincy and went on to become a Board Certified Chaplain through the Assn. of Professional Chaplains. She holds masters degrees in Rabbinic Studies and Journalism; her first career was as a newspaper and magazine editor. She speaks and teaches on end-of-life and cultural topics, and her Torah columns appear regularly in the L.A. Jewish Journal.

Rick Light has been teaching spiritual development in various ways for more than 30 years and has been studying and practicing meditation for more than 40 years. He also teaches backpacking, rock climbing, and other outdoor skills. He is a leader in the community of those who prepare Jewish bodies for burial, has published three books in this regard, and for 18 years was President of a local *Chevrah Kadisha* he started in 1996. He is a Vice President of the North American educational organization, *Kavod v'Nichum* (Honor and Comfort, see Jewish-Funerals.org), a life-long student of the Gamliel Institute, and continues to teach and raise awareness about Jewish death and burial practices at the local, state, and national levels.

About Kavod v'Nichum and Gamliel Institute

Kavod v'Nichum (KvN) is Judaism's most comprehensive end-of-life education and training organization. Its mission is to support Jewish death and bereavement practice, including the traditions and values of honoring the dead (*kavod hameit*) and comforting the bereaved (*nichum aveilim*).

KvN advocates a return to an authentic and communal Jewish response toward illness, death, burial, and mourning. This work includes strengthening individual and community efforts to organize caring communities and *chevrah kadisha* groups and helping those groups to adapt the traditions in new and meaningful ways. KvN also works to protect bereaved families from commercial exploitation around funeral and burial.

Kavod v'Nichum began its work in November of 2000 as a North American educational non-profit. It was named one of North America's top 50 innovative Jewish organizations in the ninth annual *Slingshot Guide* released on October 24, 2013. Selected from among hundreds of finalists reviewed by 83 professionals with expertise in grant-making and Jewish communal life, *Kavod v'Nichum's* work is seen as "timely, unique and ubiquitous [in an] area of concern that is overlooked by most in our community." Organizations selected were evaluated on their innovative approach, the impact of their work, leadership they have in their sector and their effectiveness at achieving results.

Kavod v'Nichum sponsors an annual international conference whose focus is on *chevrah kadisha*, Jewish cemeteries, and all aspects of Jewish death practices. These conferences have touched thousands of people. KvN's website (www.jewish-funerals.org) has extensive information on Jewish funerals, burial, and mourning. Contact KvN (info@jewish-funerals.org) if you'd like assistance in organizing a *chevrah kadisha* in your community, or if you have questions regarding any aspect of Jewish death-related practices.

KvN also sponsors the Gamliel Institute, a groundbreaking and world-class academic institution dedicated to educating and training leaders in the creation of a holistic end-of-life care continuum for their local communities. The Institute began in 2010, with the goals of deepening future leaders' Jewish knowledge and helping them experience the emotional, transformative, and spiritual aspects of *chevrah kadisha* work. More information about Gamliel can be found on the KvN website.

Other Books by the Authors

Rites of Death
The Beauty and Power of Jewish Tradition
By Richard A. Light

This book is an introduction to an inter-world space, the boundary where death and life meet: the "space between worlds" that we encounter when we deal with the dead. We enter into it through a series of extraordinary processes in which the physical actions, the prayers, and the *kavanah* involved in Jewish death rituals open a window to us a glimpse of this unique boundary. We can feel the experience of helping souls move from this world to the next through personal accounts as this book explores the practices and rituals of the Jewish tradition in preparing the dead for burial. It is an invitation to touch the fine line separating realms of existence.

Why should we put ourselves in the decidedly uncomfortable position of coming face to face with mortality? For those who engage in Jewish death rituals, that question is analogous to asking why we should see the Grand Canyon or a magnificent sunset firsthand. Helping a soul move between realms of existence inspires us, cultivates wonder, and expands our spiritual awareness. This book is dedicated to that liminal arena allowing us to peek through the doorway to heaven.

ISBN: 978-1-938288-55-5

To Midwife A Soul
Guidelines for Performing Taharah
By Richard A. Light

Expanded 4th Edition
With Chants by Rabbi Shefa Gold

This manual is a guide for those who perform the holy ritual of *taharah*, preparation of Jewish deceased for burial. Written for the *Chevrah Kadisha* of Northern New Mexico, a *chevra* that includes six shuls that differ extensively in their levels of observance, this manual is intended for use by any community. It is for all Jews. Earlier editions have been popular in the U.S. since the early 2000's, and in England since 2008.

This 4th Edition is specially formatted for ease of use in the *taharah* room as well as for education and teaching. Music has long been known to enhance the beauty and *kavanah* of the ritual. This edition is unique in that it includes the musical chanting notations of the Hebrew chant scholar, Rabbi Shefa Gold. An essential resource to those who help midwife souls from this world to the next, this book is a beautiful contribution to the field.

ISBN-10: 1489574638
ISBN-13: 978-1489574633

Final Kindness: Honoring *K'rovei Yisrael*
Burial Preparation for Non-Jews Who Are Part of The Jewish Community
By Richard A. Light

In today's modern Jewish society we are faced with an increasing number of interfaith families in which one spouse is Jewish and the other is not. When the Jewish spouse requests that their non-Jewish loved-one be buried as a Jew, a dilemma arises. How does one prepare a non-Jew for burial using Jewish traditions? Many *chevrot* and synagogues simply deny the request, stating that Jewish practices are for Jews only. Yet with so many families now expressing interest in this, it is time to create a new ritual. This book is the first of its kind in the field of Jewish death rituals, and extends the scope of the current Jewish umbrella under which our dead are respectfully prepared for burial. Every *Chevrah Kadisha* needs to be ready to handle the changing times of today's world, and thus, every community in which there are mixed-religion marriages needs this manual.

ISBN: 1484880161
ISBN-13: 9781484880166

Selected Bibliography

Traditional *Taharah* manuals:

- Epstein, Mosha. *Taharah Manual of Practices, Including Halacha Decisions of Hagaon Harav Moshe Feinstein, zt'l.* Bridgeport, CT: 1995.

- Kelman, Stuart, and Fendel, Dan. *Chesed Shel Emet, The Truest Act of Kindness.* 3rd Edition, Berkeley, CA: EKS Publishing, 2013. (Includes extensive discussion of *taharah* liturgy.)

- Light, Richard A. *To Midwife A Soul, Guidelines for Performing Tahara.* 4th Edition, Santa Fe, NM: Chevra Kadisha of Northern New Mexico, 2013. (Includes chants by Rabbi Shefa Gold.)

- Sandler-Phillips, Regina L. *PSJC Hevra Kadisha Taharah Manual.* 2nd Edition, Brooklyn, NY: Park Slope Jewish Center, 2009.

- Schlingenbaum, Yechezkel. *Taharah Guide, Prepared for the New Haven Chevrah Kadisha.* New Haven, CT: 1991.

Alternative manuals:

For washing and honoring non-Jews, based on Jewish custom:
- Light, Richard A. *Final Kindness: Honoring K'rovei Yisrael, Burial Preparation of Non-Jews Who Are Part of the Jewish Community.* Santa Fe, NM: Chevra Kadisha of Northern New Mexico, 2013.

For interfaith Home Funeral ritual:

- Final Passages' Guidebook, CREATING HOME FUNERALS, available at **http://www.finalpassages.org/**

- Home Funeral Guides: Illuminating the Path, a serialized subscription eBook and commentary, available at **http://afterdeathhomecare.com/ebook/**

- How-to Home Funeral brochure: **http://www.fca-calif.org/homefunerals.indd.pdf**

Historical works that discuss Jewish death practices:

- Eliach, Yaffa. *There Once Was a World – A 900-year Chronicle of the Shtetl of Eishyshok*, Little Brown & Co., 1998.
- Marcus, Jacob R., *Communal Sick-Care in the German Ghetto*. Hebrew Union College Press, 1978.

Traditional and contemporary trends in Jewish after-death rituals:

- Berman, Rochel U. *Dignity Beyond Death: The Jewish Preparation for Burial*. NY: Urim Publications, 2005.

- Dzmura, Noach (Editor). *Balancing on the Mechitza: Transgender in Jewish Community*. Berkeley, CA: North Atlantic Books, 2010.

- Gold, Shefa. *The Magic of Hebrew Chant: Healing the Spirit, Transforming the Mind, Deepening Love*. Woodstock, VT: Jewish Lights Publishing, 2013.

- Lamm, Maurice. *The Jewish Way in Death and Mourning*. NY: Johathan David, 1969.

- Library of the Jewish Theological Seminary of America. *From This World to the Next*. NY: JTS, 1999.

- Raphael, Simcha Paull, *Jewish Views of the Afterlife*. 2nd Edition. Lanham, MD: Rowman & Littlefield Publishers, 2009.

Websites of interest:

- Kavod v'Nichum, offers a rich resource for articles, brochures, manuals and more on Jewish death practices: **http://jewish-funerals.org**
- National Home Funeral Alliance: **http://www.homefuneralalliance.org**
- Green Burial Council: **http://greenburialcouncil.org**
- Funeral Consumers Alliance: **http://www.fca-calif.org**